The Globally Competent School: a manual

Dr Helen Wright

ISBN: 9781687567727

First published in 2019 by Dr Helen Wright

Imprint: Independently published in the UK
Edited by Sofi Freijeiro-Armitage
Images and cover by Calum Murray
Additional research by Emily Ruuskanen
Website by Serena Battistoni

www.globalcompetence.net

For the teachers and school leaders of the world

With special thanks to my global network of colleagues and all of our young people – the future is theirs to shape, and our role is to help them in this quest.

About the author

Dr Helen Wright is a well-known commentator on education and a highly experienced former school principal, having led schools in the UK and Australia for over 13 years. Since 2014 she has worked predominantly in the field of international education, driven by her belief in the importance of global competence, and she now supports numerous schools, school groups and school leaders across the globe, helping them to become the very best version of themselves, and to make a positive difference in the world.

Her international experience combines with her incisive focus on education to form a vision of the transformative power of education for all – locally, nationally and globally. In everything she does, Oxford-educated Dr Wright believes firmly and unwaveringly in the power of human beings – especially our young people - to change the world for the better.

As a qualified executive coach, she challenges leaders – not only in the world of education – to think ambitiously about the direction of their organisations, and to release the power within them to effect change. She is a non-executive chair, director and advisory board member on a number of boards in the UK and overseas, including ed-tech start-ups.

Most importantly, she derives great joy from inspiring individuals and organisations to create original and innovative strategic and practical solutions to challenging problems.

Contents

INTRODUCTION

This manual demonstrates how schools can solve the problem of how to place global competence at the heart of their work.

In my 2016 book, *Powerful Schools: how schools can be drivers of social and global mobility*, I explored why global mobility - global competence, in other words - was fundamental to extending the choices available to our young people in their lives, and therefore to increasing their social mobility and their employability. I encouraged schools to adopt a number of practical measures to embed international or global thinking into their curriculum; in fact, I devoted almost half the book to concrete examples of how to do this.

Over the past few years, working with school leaders and schools across the world, from Australia to Asia and Europe, I have seen the need for global competence become ever more pressing, and yet very few schools are embracing global competence at the heart of their curriculum, or are empowering every single student to become truly globally competent.

Given that - as I will explore in Section 1 of this book - global competence is fundamental to extending the life choices of our students, then arguably schools are negligent in their duties if they do not make the development of global competence almost their very *raison d'être*. This is why this manual is so urgent.

This manual distils my practical learnings of the past few years, drawing together a clear rationale and a very simple but powerful set of steps that schools can take -

immediately - to help their students develop into globally competent young adults.

The three sections will walk you through the journey that schools need to lead in their communities if they are to turn global competence from idea to reality:

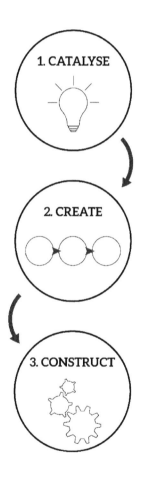

Before any school leader or teacher - or student - can do anything to make change happen in school, a fire needs to be lit. When we believe something is important, we will do it; when the imperative for change becomes so strong that we cannot imagine a future without it, then nothing can stand in our way.

For global competence to move to centre stage in school, and to become the beating heart of the school, it needs the community to be energised and invigorated in the pursuit of this goal.

Catalysing the community – in school and beyond - means capturing hearts and minds. It involves providing such an irrefutable argument for the power of global competence that it would be inconceivable for anyone to think or imagine otherwise.

This is what this section is all about.

What has global competence ever done for me?

Before you start reading this book, answer this question:

What have I gained as a result of my own global competence?

Write down everything you have gained from:

- your travels
- meeting people from different cultures
- developing diverse networks of friends and colleagues
- learning about difference and sameness in the world
- speaking other languages
- understanding what is going on in the world
- learning how to do things differently, in different places and at different times, and navigating the ways of others.

Read back to yourself what you have written, and reflect. Now consider ... why *wouldn't* you wish all of this – and more - for every single young person on this planet?

This is where global competence will take them, and this is where you, as a leader from within your school, will be able to make an enormous difference in their lives.

You may wish that you personally could be more globally competent; in fact, this journey towards global competence is for everyone, and as you create more opportunities for your students, you will also create more for your colleagues and the rest of the school community.

Every journey, after all, as the ancient Chinese proverb teaches us, begins with a first step.

Why is global competence so important?

We live in a global world. We all know this, and we have come to expect that we hear within moments of their occurrence about news events that happen halfway across the globe. We expect to be able to travel to every corner of the compass - although we are more and more mindful of doing so in a way that does not damage our planet. We do not blink at the thought that a message sent digitally can pop up on a screen anywhere in the world in a few nanoseconds. We are connected as never before: in 2016, Facebook estimated that the 'six degrees of separation' posited by Frigyes Karinthy in 1929 had reduced significantly, and that each of us is only 3.56 people-connections away from anyone else. In fact, the figure is probably lower than this now. Given that we are a global population of over 7 billion living human beings, this is quite some feat.

Just because we are physically able to communicate with anyone else, however, does not mean that we know how to do so. It does not mean that we appreciate or respect their difference from us, as well as their similarity. And when we do not communicate well, we know the outcomes: suspicion, inequality, conflict. Learning to understand others, to value cultural and linguistic difference, and to find ways to communicate, work and live together ... these are more pressing matters now than ever before, especially in light of the global issues which face us all, and which require collective global solutions.

But there is more.

No mass school system has ever been perfect, or - despite the efforts of pioneers such as John Dewey 100 years ago - truly child-centred. This is largely because, until now, schools, in all honesty, would have been doing many of their students a disservice if they really, really encouraged them to be their unique selves. Schools try, of course, and I know of no teacher who wants all children to be the same, but there lurks in all of us the fear that if students turn out to be 'too' unique, then they will not fit in, or be able to benefit from the options for further study and careers which are currently open to them.

Global competence widens these opportunities.

Global competence means that every young person can be who they really are, pursuing their interests and building on their strengths, to the point where they are in possession of a strong, confident, unique profile. Their mental and emotional health depends on this opportunity to be authentically them, of course. And we know now, at this point in history, that if they know how to access and work with anyone, anywhere in the world, then they really can justify being themselves – because someone, somewhere in this world, will want who they are and what they can offer, and they will be able to thrive and survive as a result. All they need is to be globally competent.

And there is still more.

Global competence provides the answer to inequality of opportunity in the world. Digital connection is a great leveller - free, accessible, intuitive; every young person with access to a smartphone has the tools to be able to communicate, connect, collaborate ... they simply need the opportunities, and the guidance to make the most of these opportunities. When you can access the world from even the most deprived place, urban or rural, then barriers to opportunity start to melt away ... but without the skills of robust global competence, these barriers will remain.

Schools are mandated by society to provide opportunities for young people. Examination systems - while providing pathways for many who have refined their exam techniques, and who work hard – will, if we pause to think about it, never enable every single child to excel, and can in fact potentially disenfranchise, dishearten and undermine the confidence and sense of self-worth of countless thousands each year. This is because we cannot conceive of a situation in society where we will actually allow every child to gain an 'A' or top grade – we would rather change the examinations, believing that they were not difficult enough, than permit this to happen. Examinations are not the final solution to social mobility.

Yet if we develop in young people the skills of global competence, and we find ways to enable them to become the best of themselves, then we really give them genuinely equal opportunities.

Global competence is the means to this equality of opportunity.

Global competence needs to sit at the heart of each and every school.

But what is global competence?
PISA and beyond

Put very, very simply, at its core:

Global competence is the ability to be able to understand and engage with anyone, anywhere.

This ability to be globally competent embraces a number of other dispositions, including, for example:

- knowing and constantly learning about what is happening in the world, both globally and in other countries or cultures.
- valuing other people's cultures and difference, as well as seeing their similarities to our own – and, in order to do this, building a sense of identity of self – who am I? Where have I come from? How do I see the world, and why?
- being able to converse in other languages – not every language, of course (we are not expecting the impossible of our students), but having enough of an understanding of language to appreciate that the world looks different through different linguistic constructs.
- being digitally confident, in order to be able to communicate effectively across the world – and having the skills to collaborate, negotiate, discuss, and weigh up action critically.
- having the confidence to take action – from simply reaching out to others, to being able to travel, and to acting to take personal and collective responsibility for sustainability in the world.

One of the best ways of coming to an appreciation of global competence is to spend time reflecting with colleagues on what global competence really means for you, in your school and your community, and to create your own, meaningful, context-specific model, using the language which you know will inspire your community and hit home. Just like the exercise with which you started this manual, you can use the exercise below as a reflective process to do precisely that.

What does global competence mean to us?

If you want to start this reflective process with a blank sheet and a simple question, do. If you want to revert to an existing source of expert reflection as your starting point, one of the most useful is the OECD definition of global competence, which has been developed into a framework for assessment in the new global PISA tests for global competence (the existence of which is a very clear sign that the world of education is waking up to the importance of global competence). OECD draws on years of research to define global competence as a multi-dimensional capacity:

"Globally competent individuals can …

- examine local, global and intercultural issues;
- understand and appreciate different perspectives and world views;
- interact successfully and respectfully with others; and
- take responsible action toward sustainability and collective wellbeing."

(Schleicher & Belfali, 2018: 4)

In the same report, OECD is very direct in saying why young people today need global competence:

- to live harmoniously in multicultural communities;
- to thrive in a changing labour market;
- to use media platforms effectively and responsibly;
- to support the UN's 2030 Sustainable Development Goals.

This (especially the last point) is a powerful vision … if you were tempted to think, when reading the list of what globally competent individuals should be able to do, that your school already does fairly well against all of these criteria, then stop - and restart by thinking really, really ambitiously for our young people. They are the ones who are charged with saving the planet, after all, and they won't be doing this by themselves, as individuals. They need to learn to work with others, and these 'others' will have a range of different cultural backgrounds and experiences of the world.

You may well have enough already to start igniting the process in school of coming up with your own, really challenging, definition of what global competence means, explaining it in a way that clarifies that it is a work in progress, but if you like to use existing frameworks to get you started, take a look at the Council of Europe (2016) framework, which drew on 101 schemes across the world that attempted to describe global, intercultural and/or civic skills.

What resulted was an overarching framework that underpins the OECD framework:

- knowledge about the world and other cultures
- skills to understand the world and take action (ie cognitive, communication and socio-emotional skills, including reasoning, conflict management and adaptability)
- attitudes of openness, respect for people from different cultural backgrounds, and global mindedness
- valuing human dignity and diversity.

(All of these resources can be found in the Resources List at the end of this manual.)

Take action!

Create a Professional Learning Community in your school to:

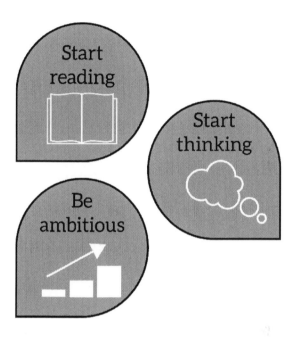

... and draw up your own, **simple but utterly clear and ambitious framework for global competence.**

It will only be a starting point, and it will shift and change over the months and years ahead, but the sooner you can commit to something in visual form, the sooner you will start to bring your community together.

**Catalysing takes energy and time –
but it is worth it.**

Tempted to teach to the test ...?
PISA won't give you all the answers

The PISA assessment of global competence (assessed for the first time in 2018) currently has 2 elements:

- cognitive assessment
- student questionnaire

The cognitive assessment tests skills such as critical thinking and whether students recognise different perspectives and influences.

The student questionnaire is more akin to background information-gathering, asking students to what extent they are familiar with global issues, and exploring their attitudes to other cultures, as well as seeking evidence about what kinds of opportunities schools are providing to develop global competence.

Alongside the assessment is a Global Competence Readiness Index for Schools – an online questionnaire which helps schools to see to what extent they are falling into line with PISA expectations. (See the Resources list at the end of this manual, where it is listed as AFS Global Competence Readiness Index for Schools. It will add to your understanding – and anything that develops this will most likely be of use to you.)

Remember, though, 3 things:

1. the PISA tests do not assess values – they are very open about this, and recognise that this is beyond the scope of (probably) any assessment tool at the moment.

Values, however, are incredibly important in the development of global competence, and as a school you will need to work out how best to develop these, extending what you no doubt already do.

2. the PISA tests do not emphasise the importance of a whole school central focus on global competence; PISA is of necessity more detached from this. The premise of this manual is that global competence needs to be absolutely at the heart of a re-orientated school, influencing its vision, mission, values and direction; PISA just takes a look and comments on what is going on, rather than driving change ... you will need to take charge of this yourselves in school.

3. PISA exists to help governments see how they are faring nationally against other governments. There is therefore a perverse argument that schools who want their governments to invest more in global competence, so as not to suffer the ignominy of coming last in the tables, should do their very best to 'fail' the tests, as this might galvanise government action ... This will of course not help young people.

It is too early to tell whether PISA 2018 (results published in December 2019) will have impact, and if so, what that impact will be. What is really significant about the PISA tests is that they are happening at all, ie that almost 30 countries in the world have signed up to gain an insight into how their young people are evolving in terms of global competence, and how this compares to young people in other parts of the world.

You have an advantage in your school, however – you have direct access to young people, and the opportunity to shift your focus and curriculum so that you can have a powerful impact on them.

You can also lead the way for others. Take all the learnings you can from PISA and from OECD, because they have done a good job of gathering together current thinking about what a global competence framework should look like.

But do not stop there – evolve these ideas (being careful not to water them down …) and work tirelessly in and with your school community to establish them at the core of your activity.

Section 2: CREATE will show you how …

The power of the 'aha' moment

One more insight, however, before you move to Section 2: CREATE.

I have found when working with leaders and teachers that the most crucial moment in the CATALYSE phase is when the penny suddenly drops, and it suddenly becomes crystal clear that global competence absolutely has to sit at the very heart of school, and must drive its vision. This is the power of the 'aha' moment – it doesn't mean that there won't be challenges in the CREATE and CONSTRUCT phases (many of which, as we will see, can be solved by finding ways to return to the CATALYSE stage), but the power that is released from the 'aha' moment will set the school on the right course.

If what you have read and understood so far in this manual hasn't yet unleashed that 'aha' moment, then try this:

Between 1986 and 2013, Milton J Bennett developed and refined a scale that reflected how we understand our relationships with others, and experience the difference of others: his Developmental Model of Intercultural Sensitivity. Starting with ethnocentrism at one end and moving to ethnorelativism at the other, this scale describes the stages each of us takes through cultural awareness:

Denial	Defence	Minimaisation		Acceptance	Adaptation	Integration
Ethnocentrism ⟶			Tipping Point	⟶ Ethnorelativism		

Adapted from Bennett, M.J. (2013)

This is really encouraging and clear – as teachers, when we see a clear pathway through learning, or when we see skills building on other skills to lead towards a more comprehensive goal, we can get quite excited, because we know where children need to go, and we know that we can help them do this.

What is <u>most</u> exciting about this scale, however, is that **it is unidirectional**. It is a one-way street; once you have learned that other cultures exist, you cannot unlearn this. Once you have realised the benefits of learning how to respect and interact in harmony with others, **there is no going back**.

In a world with global issues, which will only be solved with global cooperation, the world needs schools to develop in young people the ability to engage in harmonious intercultural relationships.

Knowing that this is not only desirable, but also eminently possible **and irreversible**, can be the 'aha' moment that school leaders and teachers often need to become excited and passionate enough about global competence to re-organise their work in schools to focus on this.

In other words, in actual fact there is no choice, and no other way to turn - schools **can** and **must** make global competence their driving force.

Pause and think ...

Before you move on to Section 2: CREATE, you need to be sure that there is a groundswell of understanding in the school community about the importance - urgency, even - of placing global competence at the heart of the school curriculum.

Make sure you have really absorbed and understood the messages in this section, and make sure that you have taken – and continue to take – really effective action:

- *inspire your community about the ideas - you will know what it takes to do this, but you can also invest in external coaching and guidance to take you through the process;*
- *connect with educators around the world online, and share your ambitions;*
- *bring challenging and inspiring speakers into school;*
- *organise whole school professional development;*
- *set up professional learning communities who will act as ambassadors and champions;*
- *lead the way in your region by creating cluster groups, organising meet-ups, or scheduling a conference on this theme.*

When you know you have enough buy-in to tip the balance, then – full steam ahead - embark on Section 2: CREATE.

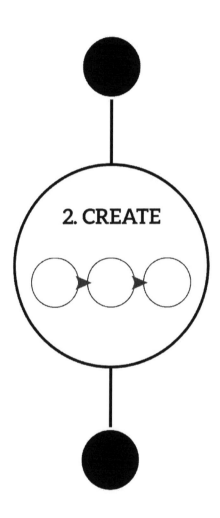

2. CREATE

Once your community understands, deeply, the imperative of developing global competence, there is no going back. You may need to keep stoking the fire, in case the urgency becomes blunted by the many other calls on the time and attention of your colleagues, so keep alert.

Set up a steering group to move the school to the next phase, and do not be afraid to invest in external supervision or coaching to hold you to account. This can be incredibly effective in ensuring that you do what you set out to do.

You can now turn your attention to the next phase – creating a model and framework that will scaffold the construction that is to come.

Every school is, of course, different, but this section sets out a prototype model that will serve as a starting point for this next step.

The 3 Levels of a Globally Competent School

This is the model I share with schools with which I work. It has 3 Levels: **Level 1: Foundations; Level 2: Developing; Level 3: Established.** As you read the next few pages, note the strong directional movements within this model:

- a move from an **understanding** of the importance of global competence to a **communal commitment**, genuinely shared by the entire community (i.e. not just a mission statement on the wall), and then to a **communal passion**, where the entire community feels a sense of personal responsibility to create and sustain opportunities for young people to develop global competence – as well as for their teachers and leaders, because they need to drive this passion.

- a move in the curriculum from **learning about** different cultures and different parts of the world, towards **learning alongside** people with different perspectives on the world, followed by a move towards **genuine experiential learning**, practising walking in others' shoes and seeing the world through their eyes.

- a move from using technology to **inform** – e.g. research to find out what is going on in the world – to using technology to **connect** with others in different parts of the world, and then really **engage**, so that students begin to see it as entirely normal and possible to work through video-conference and in person with their counterparts across the globe. Connections may initially be exploratory; engagement, when it is fully in place, will manifest itself as continual, natural, genuine, respectful communication.

Level 1: Foundations

Global Awareness

A school which is operating at *Level 1: Foundations* will be able to demonstrate strong **Global Awareness** in school, including:

- a visible communal <u>understanding</u> that global competence for all students is important;
- curriculum coverage of international and global issues (e.g. geographical, historical, political and literary);
- co-curricular interest groups (e.g. languages clubs, debating societies, charitable action groups etc);
- community involvement in international festivals;
- regular use of technology to <u>inform</u> understanding (e.g. exploring and researching topics).

Note that many schools do this very well – the curriculum in most schools, in fact, provides a sound framework for the development of knowledge and skills that support global competence.

What does this mean for us?

Level 2:
Developing

Global Relationships

A school which is operating at *Level 2: Developing* will be able to demonstrate strong **Global Relationships** in school, including:

- a visible communal <u>commitment</u> to extending opportunities to develop global competence for all;
- programmes designed to develop global competence;
- regular visits to the school by groups from other cultures (e.g. teachers, students, cultural groups);
- opportunities for all students to engage in international visits, exchanges and longer-term international stays;
- active development of networks to provide global access for students (e.g. work experience, mentoring);
- regular use of technology to <u>connect</u> (e.g. with students from different countries and cultures).

Note that while many schools offer plenty of opportunities, far from all schools offer extensive and comprehensive opportunities for all students.

What does this mean for us?

Level 3:
Established

Global Partnerships

A school which is operating at *Level 3: Established* will be able to demonstrate strong **Global Partnerships** in school, including:

- a visible communal <u>passion</u> for extending opportunities to develop global competence for all;
- teaching and learning of global competence embedded into the curriculum and co-curriculum, with clear outcomes and expectations;
- prolific engagement – virtual and in person - by all students and teachers with established networks, including schools and organisations across the world;
- a dedicated campus or partner school – or, preferably, more than one – in another part of the world, to provide reciprocal opportunities for students;
- regular use of technology to <u>engage</u> (eg in collaboration and co-working, and in co-constructing curriculum).

What does this mean for us?

An honest audit

This model paints a picture, and starts to build a structure within which schools can create their own context-specific model. One of the most important first steps towards this is to do an honest audit of where your school currently sits within the model.

When I first started working with schools on global competence, I asked colleagues to audit the opportunities that they provided for students that would enable them to develop global competence, but I (and they) very quickly realised that this task obscured the reality of the situation. A school can demonstrate that it offers a plethora of opportunities – debating in Year 7, for instance, or an exchange to Germany in Year 10, or international work experience for language students in Year 12, or visits by global universities to a careers fair in Year 11 … all of these are worthy initiatives, but the real question is … **what is the experience of each and every student**, throughout their time in the school?

The opportunities provided in school to develop global competence need to support the <u>sustained</u> development of the child's skills, attitudes and values, in much the same way as we expect the opportunities for a child to learn Maths in school to support a sustained development in Maths skills for every child. To continue the analogy, we put a lot of effort in schools into structuring Maths programmes, ensuring that every student has adequate time to develop Maths skills at the pace which suits them, then assessing their Maths skills, providing differentiated interventions if necessary, and generally ensuring that young people do not leave school without a good basic ability in Maths, and the confidence to use Maths in the world.

Global competence is as important as Maths, and it deserves the same kind of attention.

Part of the strong directional movement illustrated in the model of the Levels of a globally competent school requires schools to ensure that students themselves have a strong directional movement through their school career in developing their global competence.

Access to a few voluntary activities, sprinkled sparsely throughout their time in the school, just does not cut it. Young people deserve better.

So ... the first step is to audit, honestly and thoroughly, the experience of the child in school.

What does an audit look like?

Take a typical student in your school and think about the opportunities that they have had to develop global competence in every stage of their career to date (and ahead of them).

Write down everything you know – and ask your colleagues for help. What did they learn in Geography that might help them become more globally competent? Or in English?

What do they do and learn that will support their global competence?

	Knowledge	Skills	Attitudes
Pre-K/K/ Nursery			
Year 1			
Year 2			
Year 3			
Year 4			
Year 5			
Year 6			
Year 7			
Year 8			
Year 9			
Year 10			
Year 11			
Year 12			
Year 13			

Do this for a number of different students, including students who have moved into the school at different times – you know that mobility is increasing, and students will be entering your school with different educational backgrounds.

Can you see any patterns?

Is there any developmental consistency?

Where are the gaps?

Now do this exercise again – if you were going to assess yourself as a school against the experience of this student, or these students, how would you rate yourself: as a Level 1, Level 2, or Level 3 school?

Use traffic light colours for maximum visual effect:

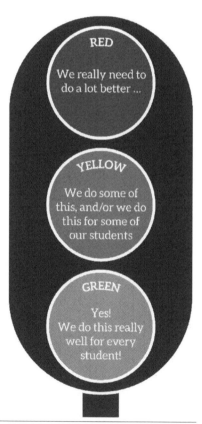

RED
We really need to do a lot better ...

YELLOW
We do some of this, and/or we do this for some of our students

GREEN
Yes!
We do this really well for every student!

Where are we in developing global competence in our students? Are we a …			
	Level 1 School: Foundations?	Level 2 School: Developing?	Level 3 School: Established?
Pre-K/K/ Nursery			
Year 1			
Year 2			
Year 3			
Year 4			
Year 5			
Year 6			
Year 7			
Year 8			
Year 9			
Year 10			
Year 11			
Year 12			
Year 13			

What have you learned from this exercise?

What are you going to do next?

A word of caution – if your sheet looks very green, then – and I say this with the greatest of respect, and in the desire to help you - you are most likely fooling yourself ...! Go back to Section 1 and re-read it ... do you and your community really, really understand what global competence can look like? Are your students genuinely globally competent, and if so, how do you know?

One of the most powerful learnings I had in this sphere was when I realised that underneath the apparent confidence of so many of our students lies an anxiety and lack of inner self-confidence – a natural uncertainty about the unknown - born of the fact that they have not had enough opportunity to build the robustness in global competence that they have in, say, writing examination papers ...

Watch out for your own complacency ... and don't always believe your own marketing hype as a school ...

Global competence is too important simply to gloss over ... be honest, and then you will understand your starting point on the pathway towards construction of a structure that really, really works for young people.

What gets in the way of developing global competence?

We need to be realistic: the path towards global competence will not always be straightforward. Global competence is so obviously the right thing to develop that we can very easily use the language of global citizenship, global mobility, global awareness etc, but in practice diminish their impact.

Any school which bristles at the thought that it is anything but 'globally ready' probably needs to look very closely at itself ... and work out what is making its community so defensive.

Hurdles to the development of global competence come in many forms. Some of these are issues which we can help young people overcome – skills development, for example; read the list on the next page through the lens of the teacher or parent first, however.

If the adults around a young person are not convinced about the necessity of global competence in the world, how can we expect the young person to be?

So ... what gets in the way of our students when they seek to develop global competence?

Psychological
- Negative or suspicious attitudes and experiences ...
- ... of parents and families
- ... prevalent in society (media etc)
- ... of teachers (yes, even teachers)

Skills
- Lack of digital skills
- Lacks of linguistic skills
- Lack of intercultural skills
- Lack of social/emotional skills, especially self-confidence

Practical
- Poor technological connections
- Costs (of travel, especially)
- Opportunities to connect and experience

Perhaps you can add more hurdles to the list... The real task, however, is to answer the question of how you are going to address these hurdles, especially with parents and the wider community.

The answer lies, neatly, not just in the CATALYSE phase, to which you may need to return, but also in the CONSTRUCT phase.

Pause and think ...

Before you move on to Section 3: CONSTRUCT, stop for a moment and consider the following:

- *How well is everything going? Are more and more people in the community really, really passionate about finding new ways to help students — all students — become truly globally competent?*

- *Do you need to inject some more momentum into your quest to be the globally competent school? Do you need to return to Section 1: CATALYSE for a while, and do some more catalysing?*

- *Now that your steering group has been working together for some time, are they the right people? Are they delivering? Can you see evidence of their impact?*

Global competence is too important to let fade.

If things aren't yet right, do something different — change the people, change the processes, spend more time convincing people of the need to put global competence firmly in the centre of school activity.

Set your mind to this ... and do whatever it takes to make it happen.

Some of this may involve delving into Section 3: CONSTRUCT and the process of constructing further opportunities for your students ... but beware ... without a shared, strong imperative to re-orientate the school around global competence, there is a very real danger that your progress will stall, as complacency settles in ...

So ... make sure you are ready to move on to Section 3: CONSTRUCT, and do so ... but stay alert!

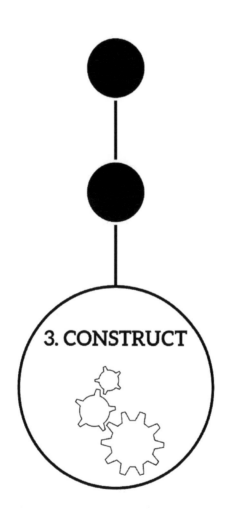

3. CONSTRUCT

It calms us as teachers and leaders sometimes to think that development planning is linear, and that with a model and an audit in place, and with a keen (and growing) awareness of the importance of global competence, we will be able to move, simply and effortlessly, to the next level of implementation.

This is not of course how schools – or any organisations, for that matter - work; school development is better conceptualised as a spiral of (hopefully) continually deepening engagement. This is particularly the case when developing global competence, because in order to do so, the school will have to reach out beyond its gates and draw in its much, much wider community.

The good news is that in drawing in others to provide opportunities for students and teachers, you will have the chance to help them understand the importance of global competence – convert them to the cause, in other words. This is the beautiful virtual circle of schools taking control of their community engagement, and this is what this next section is all about.

The power of community

In *Powerful Schools: how schools can be drivers of social and global mobility*, I explored at length how a school should be seen as a hub of a series of interrelated networks - its local, national and global community:

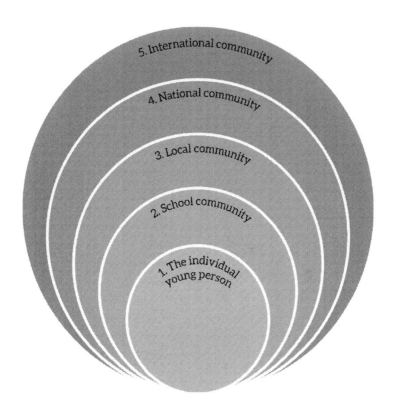

I also devoted over 90 pages in *Powerful Schools* to practical examples of how schools can engage with their stakeholders in each of these spheres of their activity. It would be daft to repeat all of these here; besides, what really matters is the true ownership of the development of global competence in your school, through the ideas and actions that come from within.

When I work with schools, my task is to ignite, not to direct – you need to own your own development … and besides, you are perfectly capable of doing so.

The capacity to grow global competence lies within **you** …

Key messages to remember:

- You cannot do everything by yourself. If you are going to provide your students with multiple opportunities to develop their global competence, in a rich and integrated programme throughout their school career, then you will need to draw on other resources outside the immediate school community.

- People you know (or who you could choose to know) in the local, national and international community have access to the opportunities that you and your students want and need; in short – these opportunities are out there.

- You can reach out to anyone – any organisation, any other school, any individual - in the world if you choose to do so … and if you do a little bit of research, you are likely to find that someone in your community has some connection with them, however distant. Use this connection – you are doing this for the sake of your students and for the better development of the world … do not hold back through some sense of social awkwardness.

- Other people generally want to help. This should not surprise you, because you probably want to help others. Just don't be afraid to ask.

And – finally …

You lose nothing by asking – and you have everything to gain!

What kind of opportunities do you want to ask for?

The 3 main categories of opportunity you will want to consider asking for are:

Access to people's experiences includes:

- Learning from people's lives. Invite people into school to hear about their life journeys – personal and professional. Think not so much about really inspiring, extraordinary people (although these people are important to hear too, for many reasons); instead, think about the business owner down the road who imports and exports services or goods over the internet, and who has learned to communicate with customers around the world. Or think about the immigrant parent who can shed light on different cultural expectations.

- Exposing students to stories of people's journeys. These do not have to be in formal lecture contexts, run by local universities (although these are valuable too, for numerous reasons); YouTube (and other curated video content) is a rich source and an opportunity to see the world through other people's eyes. Let your students explore – in fact, encourage them to do so; if you have given them a strong grounding in online digital safety, then you are opening the world to them.

- Connections ... and you cannot have too many of these, even though you will have to work out how to resource the time needed to cultivate these properly. Remember that if you don't ask, you certainly won't get ... and your students deserve every opportunity you can find for them.

A word of caution – you are trying to help shape the future, and this means improving the present ... not all the people you encounter will share the values you want to espouse in a globally competent young person.

Make sure that you are certain, before you let people loose on the minds of your students, that they understand what you want to achieve, and that they are able to articulate their experiences in this way.

Your role may well extend to catalysing their understanding too ... but herein lies one of the real beauties of the system, because by reaching out to ask for help, you are also helping to spread an education of global competence beyond the school community, and out into the world, where it needs to go.

Experiential learning includes:

- Visits to workplaces, to see language and intercultural activity in person. Note that these visits can start really, really young – Kindergarten students are immensely open to the world, and the impact of experiential learning on them is enormous. When the values associated with global competence are embedded and made explicit in these visits, the journey towards global competence later in school life becomes easier.

  It can be extremely easy to re-orientate the purpose of experiential learning to place global competence at the heart of it. A visit to a bakery, for example, can talk about the origins of different types of bread or pastry in eg France or the Lebanon, for instance, show how it is important to families, and make sure that children see on a map how far these cultural traditions have migrated.

- Work experience or work shadowing. This can be in the company down the road that sells over the internet, or it can be in an international context. The value of work experience or work shadowing speaks for itself, as long as it is well-planned, integrated into the curriculum and reflected upon carefully afterwards.

Financial support includes:

- Support for individual students and cohorts for their travel plans – travel scholarships, funded accommodation etc.

- Donations of technology equipment or software to upgrade digital connections.

- Pro-bono volunteer support in school to manage events, travel, resources, networks … anything, in fact, that you realise that you need to do additionally if you are going to make your drive to embed global competence really work.

Remember: if you don't ask, you won't receive!

So - ask!

Above all, though, remember the complacency trap … a few opportunities, however interesting, do not make for a full and integrated curriculum with global competence at its core. Stay constantly on guard against this complacency and keep checking in on your audit – does every child and young person have access to an engaging, well-grounded and well-developed programme that extends their global competence? Can you see a measurable impact that these opportunities are having on your students? What more is needed to deepen the impact?

As long as there is more still to do, your work is not yet finished...

What does the development of global competence in school look like in practice?

When it comes down to it, the pedagogies you use to develop global competence will look familiar:

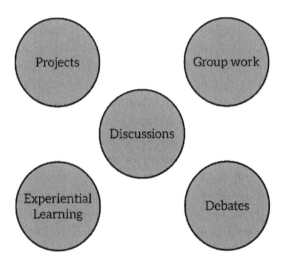

You already know that the skills of collaboration, critical and creative thinking – amongst other skills – are vital for students to develop in today's world (and as good learners generally), and you will already be working on these (to some extent, at least) in your current curriculum.

What will be different, however, when you start to focus on global competence at the core of the school's activity, will be:

- the **explicit expectations and understanding** of global competence embedded into the tasks you set;

- the **breadth and range of the contexts** within which these tasks – opportunities to learn about, understand and engage with different cultures, which extend far beyond the scope of your current curriculum;

- the **cohesion** of your approach, and the fact that it is embedded and highly visible throughout the school, **from the earliest years right through to the last year of school** ... and beyond, to your wider school community.

Now is a good time to commit to your vision for global competence in your school and create your picture of the globally competent school.

Inspired by all the thoughts and insights you have gained in the process of working through this manual, make your vision of your ideal globally competent school visible to you and to others.

Whether this is in words, pictures, music ... however you want to do this, and whoever you want to draw into the process, **just do it**.

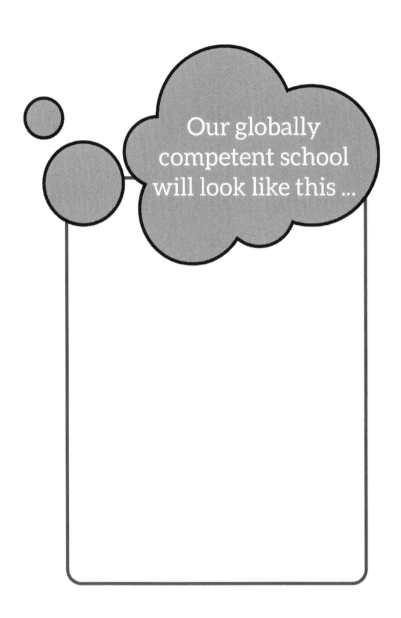

Our globally competent school will look like this ...

Is it worth preparing a 'Global Competence Programme' in school?

Yes, it is … although remember that this will only take you to a 'Level 2: Developing' school, so do not assume that once you have a programme in place, that you have cracked the nut of global competence.

Besides, if you only run it for, say, 6 weeks in Year 11, then you will fail the audit test that demands young people be exposed to, and learn about, global competence throughout their school career.

(Remember the comparison with Maths teaching? You wouldn't teach Maths for 6 weeks in Year 11 and expect your students to be competent in Maths …)

The following two models of Global Competence Programmes are based on a combined experience of programmes in schools across the world which contain some element of global competence.

Model 1 of a Global Competence Programme involves students moving in a linear fashion from background information to debate and discussion, to experiential learning.

GLOBAL COMPETENCE PROGRAMME MODEL 1:

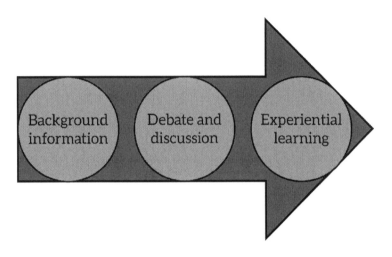

Background reading and discussion can be research-based, and/or include lectures, reading and other forms of information-gathering, on topics such as:

- human rights
- global government
- ethics
- global issues, such as climate change
- culture

(Note: if you are looking for inspiration, use the UN's Sustainable Development Goals as a great starting point.)

Debates and discussion will emerge from the background information, but will also require the development of specific skills, including:

- critical thinking, including skills of analysis, discernment and synthesis
- collaborative and team-based working
- creative and imaginative thinking
- formal debating and public speaking training
- structuring and articulating of arguments
- communication skills

Experiential learning is not yet common in Global Competence programmes, but when it does happen, it can take the form of:

- collaborative project work with peers from other countries, ideally in person in a different cultural location (or locations), but potentially also over video-conferencing
- visits or service-learning projects in a different cultural context, building on what students have learned, and/or taking the opportunity to test out hypotheses and prior assumptions
- a 'capstone' or 'symposium' – a large-scale get-together which marks a culmination of the topic

Some successful programmes take a case study approach, ie they start with the problem itself, and this is reflected in Model 2 of a Global Competence Programme.

GLOBAL COMPETENCE PROGRAMME MODEL 2:

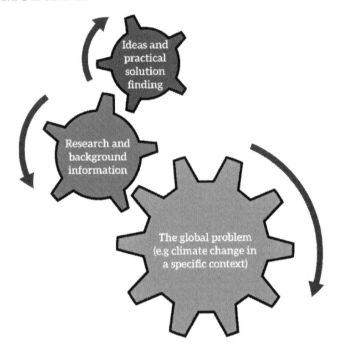

Ideas and practical solution finding

Research and background information

The global problem (e.g climate change in a specific context)

This Model covers the same areas as Model 1, but starts with a problem rather than with research and background learning. (For example, the problem might be how to solve, in an environmentally friendly way, the growing demand for electricity in Shanghai.)

Posing this problem encourages the students to explore what the scale of the problem is, and what the current situation is, which leads in turn to ideas, which can be tested through critical thinking and analysis. This often leads to a reconfiguration of the problem itself, through a deep appreciation of the connected issues.

But remember ...

Neither of these Models is sufficient to create a Globally Competent School, which is what you want to achieve.

Just because other schools have these programmes in place does not mean that this is enough.

Your role is to:

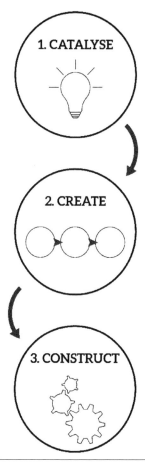

… and develop your own whole-school approach to global competence – a mindset and attitude, as much as a visible and cohesive programme.

You can do this.

FINAL WORDS AND NEXT STEPS

This manual has shown you how to:

THINK Global Competence

You understand the importance of global competence for young people, their future employability and their life choices. You have begun to see how adopting global competence at the core of a school's activity can transform education. You know the difference that global competence can make.

FEEL Global Competence

You feel the urgency and the need to do this now – global competence really, really matters for young people and their futures, and there is not a moment to waste.

DO Global Competence

You know where to start, and where to head ... you have the tools at your fingertips.

Moreover, you have learned that …

You can do it.

You <u>can</u> actually do it.

You will need to bring others together to collaborate.

And the more you can engage, the better.

But you <u>can do it</u>.

And you have the tools to do it.

And if not you, then who …?

Start today.

In this manual, I wanted to capture the early ideas and emerging realities of global competence in schools because I am passionate about the power and potential of global competence to make a fundamental difference in the lives of our young people across the world, and I wanted to share this and spread this as far and wide as possible.

I would love to share your journey with you, and hear what you achieve. If I can help you, or connect you with others, just ask.

The more we can share with one another, the more inspiration we will draw from one another, and the more we will be able to help our young people.

Keep in touch via
www.globalcompetence.net
where you can access a range of resources and contribute to a worldwide dialogue.

Together we can enable our next generation to become more globally competent.

They need this from us.

And, without sounding overly dramatic, so does the world.

So do it.

RESOURCES

Books

Bennett, M. (2013). *Basic concepts of intercultural communication: Paradigms, principles, & practices.* Boston: Intercultural Press

Berardo, K., Deardorff, D. (2012). *Building Cultural Competence: Innovative Models and Activities.* Sterling: Stylus

Byram, M. (2008). *From Foreign Language Education to Education for Intercultural Citizenship.* Clevedon: Multilingual Matters

Fennes, H. Hapgood, K. (1997). *Intercultural Learning in the Classroom: Crossing Borders.* London: Cassell

Meyer, E. (2014). *The Culture Map: Breaking Through the Invisible Boundaries of Global Business.* New York: Ingram Publisher Services

Rychen, D., Salganik, L. (eds.) (2003). *Key Competencies for a Successful Life and a Well-Functioning Society,* Gottingen: Hogrefe and Huber

Walker, A, Dimmock, C. (2005). *Educational Leadership: Culture and Diversity.* Thousand Oaks: SAGE Publications Inc.

Wright, H. (2016). *Powerful Schools: how schools can be drivers of social and global mobility.* London: John Catt

Wright, H. (2019). 'An international dimension: making a world of difference'. In Sanderson, K., Ball, C., Preedy, P. (2019). *Early Childhood Education Refined.* (pp 131-140). Abingdon: Routledge

Reports

Barrett, M., Byram, M., Lázár, I., Mompoint-Gaillard, P., Philippou, S. (2014). *Developing Intercultural Competence through Education*. Strasbourg: Council of Europe Publishing

Boix Mansilla V., Jackson, A. (2011) *Educating for Global Competence: Preparing Our Youth to Engage the World*. Asia Society and Council of Chief State School Officers.

Boix Mansilla, V. (2013). *Educating for Global Competence: Learning Redefined for an Interconnected World*. Asia Society/ Interdisciplinary Studies Project (online) Available at: http://pz.harvard.edu/sites/default/files/Educating%20for%20Global%20Competence%20Short%20HHJ.pdf [accessed 28 June 2019]

British Council (2013). *Culture at Work: The Value of Intercultural Skills in the Workplace*. UK: British Council

Council of Europe (2015). *Tasks for democracy: 60 activities to learn and assess transversal attitudes, skills, and knowledge.* Strasbourg: Council of Europe.

Council of Europe (2016). *Competence for Democratic Culture: Living Together as Equals in Culturally Diverse Democratic Societies.* Strasbourg: Council of Europe.

Deardorff, D. (2013). *Promoting understanding and development of Intercultural dialogue and peace: a comparative analysis and global perspective of regional studies on intercultural competence*, report prepared for UNESCO Division of Cultural Policies and Intercultural Dialogue. Paris: UNESCO

Institute of International Education (2017.) *A World on the Move: Trends in Global Student Mobility. IIe: The Power of International Education* (online) Available at: https://www.iie.org/Research-and-Insights/Publications/A-World-on-the-Move [accessed 13 April 2019]

Lázár, I. (2012) *Recognising Intercultural Competence: What Shows That I Am Culturally Competent?* Strasbourg: Council of Europe. Available at: http://www.coe.int/t/dg4/education/Pestalozzi/home/Wha t/ICCTool_en.asp [accessed 20 August 2019]

Lee Colvin, R. and Edwards, V. (2018). *Teaching for Global Competence in a Rapidly Changing World.* Asia Society – Center for Global Education (online) Available at: https://asiasociety.org/sites/default/files/inline-files/teaching-for-global-competence-in-a-rapidly-changing-world-edu.pdf [accessed 28 June 2019]

Oxfam (2015). *Education for Global Citizenship, a guide for schools.* Oxford: Oxfam

Richard, N. Lowe, R. Hanks, C. (2015). *Gone International: Mobility Works.* Go International Programme/Universities UK International (online) Available at: https://www.universitiesuk.ac.uk/policy-and-analysis/reports/Documents/International/GoneInternationa l2017_A4.pdf [accessed 8 April 2019]

Schleicher, A. Belfali, Y. (2018). *Preparing our youth for an inclusive and sustainable world.* OECD/PISA (online) Available at: https://www.oecd.org/education/Global-competency-for-an-inclusive-world.pdf [accessed 14 May 2019]

UNESCO (2001). *Universal Declaration of Cultural Diversity.* Paris: UNESCO. Available at http://unesdoc.unesco.org/images/0012/001271/12760m.pdf

UNESCO (2007). *Guidelines on Intercultural Education.* Paris: UNESCO

UNESCO (2013). *Intercultural Competences: Conceptual and operational Framework.* Paris: UNESCO

UNESCO (2014a). *Global Citizenship Education: Preparing learners for the challenges of the 21st century.* Paris: UNESCO

UNESCO (2014b). *Learning to Live Together: Education Policies and Realities in the Asia-Pacific.* Paris: UNESCO

UNESCO (2014c). *Teaching Respect for All.* Paris: UNESCO

UNESCO (2015). *Global Citizenship Education: Topics and Learning Objectives.* Paris: UNESCO

UNESCO (2016). *Global Education Monitoring Report.* Paris: UNESCO

Articles

Anderson, E. (2007). 'Fair Opportunity in Education: A Democratic Equality Perspective.' Ethics 117, no. 4 (July 2007): 595-622. The University of Chicago (online) Available at: http://www.mit.edu/~shaslang/mprg/AndersonFOE.pdf [accessed 13 April 2019]

Bennett, M. (1986). 'A developmental approach to training for intercultural sensitivity.' International Journal of Intercultural Relations 10, no.2: 179-95

Bennett, M. (1993). 'Towards ethnorelativism: A developmental model of intercultural sensitivity.' In M. Paige (ed.), *Education for the intercultural experience.* Yarmouth, ME: Intercultural Press

Bennett, M. (2004). 'Becoming interculturally competent.' In J. Wurzel (Ed.), *Toward multiculturalism: A reader in multicultural education* (2nd ed., pp. 62-77). Newton, MA: Intercultural Resource

Boix Mansilla, V. (2016). 'How to be a global thinker', Educational Leadership, Vol.74/4, pp. 10-16

Jackson, A. (2004). 'Preparing Urban Youths to Succeed in the Interconnected World of the 21st Century.' *Phi Delta Kappa* (online) Volume 86 (no.3) Available at: https://www.jstor.org/stable/20441740 [accessed 8 April 2019]

Klein, Jennifer D. (2013). 'Making meaning in a standards-based world: Negotiating tensions in global education.' *Educational Forum* (online) Vol. 77/4, pp. 481-490, http://dx.doi.org/10.1080/00131725.2013.822044

Seelye, H.N. (1996). 'Experimental activities for intercultural learning.' Yarmouth, ME: Intercultural Press

Stringer, D., Cassidy, P. (2009). '52 Activities for Improving Cross-Cultural Communication.' Yarmouth, ME: Intercultural Press

Vander Ark, T., Liebtag, E. (2017). 'Educating for Global Competence: 6 reasons, 7 competencies, 8 strategies, 9 innovations.' Getting Smart. Available at: https://www.gettingsmart.com/2017/09/educating-for-global-competence-6-reasons-7-competencies-8-strategies-9-innovations/amp/ [accessed 29 August 2019]

Williams-Gualandi, D. (2015). 'Intercultural Understanding: What are we looking for and how do we assess what we find?' Working Papers Series: International and Global Issues for Research No. 2015/7, University of Bath

Websites

AFS Global Competence Readiness Index for Schools. (2019) (https://afs.org/index/)

Printed in Great Britain
by Amazon

34976881R00047